T0327885

From Italy:

A celebration of creativity from Italy, compiled and published by Counter-Print

First published in 2023 © Counter-Print
ISBN 978-1-915392-07-7 Designed by Counter-Print
Printed in China

With special thanks to all the contributors.

I think it fair to say that Italy is recognised as being a worldwide leader in design. The architect Luigi Caccia Dominioni claimed: 'Quite simply, we are the best' and 'We have more imagination, more culture and are better mediators between the past and the future.' Bold claims, but Italy has exerted a vast influence on urban, industrial, interior, fashion and graphic design worldwide.

We're all familiar with the top Italian brands from fashion, furniture and household products to automotive designs. Brands, such as Gucci, Bialetti, B&B Italia and Ferrari are globally renowned and offer the best that Italian design has to offer.

Modern Italian design has had a huge impact on the definition of style and elegance. However, in Italy's design spectrum, industrial design, fashion and furniture have long overshadowed graphics. This is rather unfair, given that many aspects of contemporary graphic design, not least the form of the book, have their roots in Renaissance Italy.

The word 'renaissance' means revival or rebirth. The Renaissance was a fervent period of European cultural, artistic, political and economic rebirth following the Middle Ages. Generally described as taking place from the 14th century to the 17th century, the Renaissance promoted the rediscovery of classical philosophy, literature and art. Some of the greatest thinkers, authors, statesmen, scientists and artists in human history thrived during this era, while global exploration opened up new lands and cultures to European commerce.

Importantly in the history of graphic design, the Renaissance and the work of the Italian humanists is closely bound to an innovative approach in book design. Although fifteenth century Italy was a patchwork of city-states, monarchies, republics and papal domains, it was at the height of its wealth and patronage of the arts and architecture.

Centred in Venice, Italian printers of the Renaissance made a series of design innovations to the layout of books, some of which we continue to use today. These include the title page, roman and italic type, printed page numbers, woodblock and cast metal ornaments as well as innovation in the layout of illustrations with type. In fact, Italy sponsored the first printing press to be set up outside of Germany.

Other artistic movements, such as Futurism, had large impacts on design. Futurism was originated by Filippo Marinetti in 1909. It rejected the past and set out to celebrate a number of abstract concepts like dynamism, speed, technology, youth, violence and objects such as the car, the aeroplane and the industrial city. The Futurist movement was short-lived, ending in 1916, but it influenced designers and artists all over the world. For example, in 1933, a team of progressive designers, printers and photographers started the magazine 'Campo Grafico' and Studio Boggeri was founded in Milan by the designer and photographer Antonio Boggeri as a bastion of 'International Style' graphics.

Studio Boggeri employed many of the most influential Italian designers of the day including Marcello Nizzoli, who is renowned for his work for the Italian office equipment manufacturer Olivetti and Albe Steiner, best known for his projects for radical political groups. It also forged a close relationship with many of the Italian companies, which would pioneer the commercial use of modern graphic design during the mid-20th century, including the tyre maker Pirelli as well as Olivetti. Studio Boggeri's corporate logos, advertising and other visual materials were critical to the success of these companies. Other prominent 20th century Italian graphic designers engaged with different disciplines too, like Bruno Munari, an engineer-turned-artist who also designed books and magazines. Enzo Mari started out as an artist, before turning to product design and then graphics, while A.G. Fronzoni, Alessandro Mendini and Ettore Sottsass also practiced architecture.

The vitality of Italy's graphic design scene encouraged talented foreign designers to move and work there. Max Huber moved to Milan from Switzerland to produce compelling designs for Italian companies like the retail group La Rinascente. The Dutchman Bob Noorda devised the graphic component of one of Italy's most ambitious early 1960s design projects, the Milan subway system, before teaming up with Massimo Vignelli to co-found Unimark. By the mid-1960s they had moved to New York, where their commissions included the signage for the city's subway system and, eventually, Vignelli's map. Meanwhile, in London, Germano Facetti was also a prominent figure in British book design where he worked for Penguin in the 1960s.

Italian design was pollinated around the world in the twentieth century, by the country's leading design practitioners. The international style Antonio Boggeri helped pioneer, was imbued with a distinctive playfulness, leaving an indelible mark on how we see and interact with the world around us. This 'Italian design' has been forged from innovation and technology. What we witness now is a design culture that seems independent and multi-disciplinary, offering a combination of rich tradition, craftsmanship, modernity and playfulness.

Jon Dowling
Counter-Print

Parco Studio

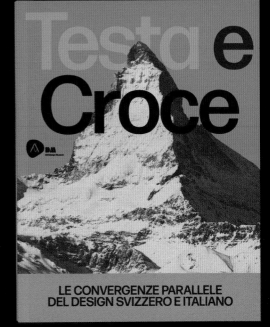

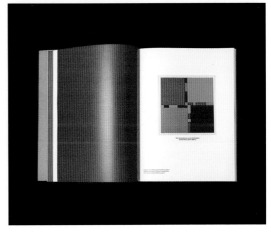

ADI, Testa e Croce

Identity for ADI Museo del
Compasso d'Oro
2022

Testa e
Croce

LE CONVERGENZE PARALLELE
DEL DESIGN SVIZZERO E ITALIANO

LE CONVERGENZE PARALLELE
DEL DESIGN SVIZZERO E ITALIANO

LE CONVERGENZE PARALLELE
DEL DESIGN SVIZZERO E ITALIANO
DAL 25.10.22 AL 05.02.23

LE CONVERGENZE PARALLELE
DEL DESIGN SVIZZERO E ITALIANO
DAL 25.10.22 AL 05.02.23

LE CONVERGENZE PARALLELE
DEL DESIGN SVIZZERO E ITALIANO
DAL 25.10.22 AL 05.02.23

LE CONVERGENZE PARALLELE
DEL DESIGN SVIZZERO E ITALIANO
DAL 25.10.22 AL 05.02.23

LE CONVERGENZE PARALLELE
DEL DESIGN SVIZZERO E ITALIANO
DAL 25.10.22 AL 05.02.23

Winifred

Identity for a cultural center

2021

Quaderni de Lacittàintorno

Editorial design
communicating urban research
in Lacittàintorno neighbourhoods
by Fondazione Cariplo
2019

→

Lacittàintorno

Identity for the Fondazione Cariplo
programme, Lacittàintorno
2017 – 2020

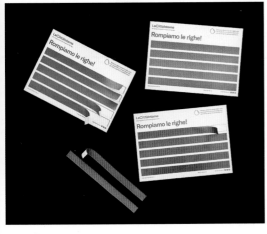

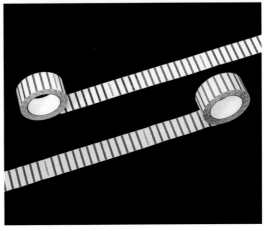

DAS RUNDE MUSS INS ECKIGE, literally "The round thing must enter the square thing" is capsule collection by Parco Studio and Palazzi.club that celebrates the desire to pursue one's goals, even when these seem impossible to achieve. Five unique pieces made original 1990s jerseys, in which everyone will recognize Nike's historic design for Borussia Dortmund, recovered from the bottom of an old English warehouse.

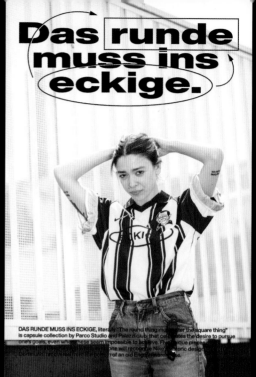

DAS RUNDE MUSS INS ECKIGE, literally "The round thing must enter the square thing" is capsule collection by Parco Studio and Palazzi.club that celebrates the desire to pursue one's goals, even when these seem impossible to achieve. Five unique pieces made original 1990s jerseys, in which everyone will recognize Nike's historic design Dortmund, recovered from the bottom of an old English warehouse.

DAS RUNDE MUSS INS ECKIGE, literally "The round thing must enter the square thing" is capsule collection by Parco Studio and Palazzi.club that celebrates the desire to pursue one's goals, even when these seem impossible to achieve. Five unique pieces made by mid 1990s jerseys, in which everyone will recognize Nike's historic design for Borussia Dortmund, recovered from the bottom of an old English warehouse.

Das Runde Muss Ins Eckige

Self-initiated capsule collection
2022

CRSL

From Italy

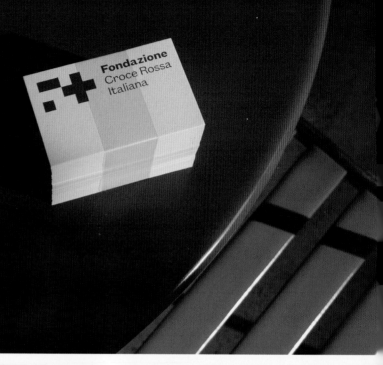

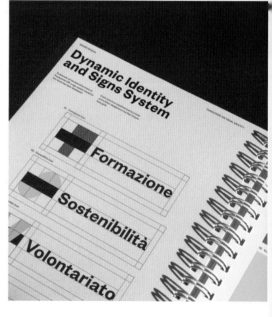

Fondazione CRI

Identity for the Italian Red Cross
2020

Modena FC 1912

Identity for a football team

2022

Vitoni Spritz
Identity & packaging design
for a beverage company
2021

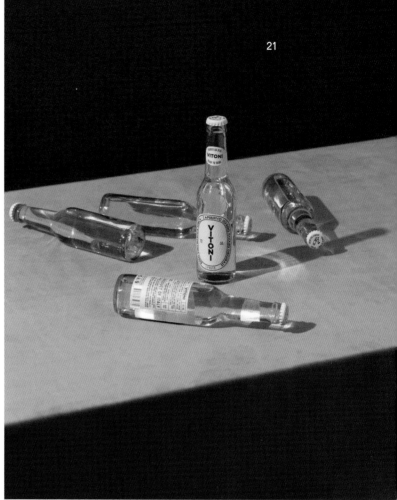

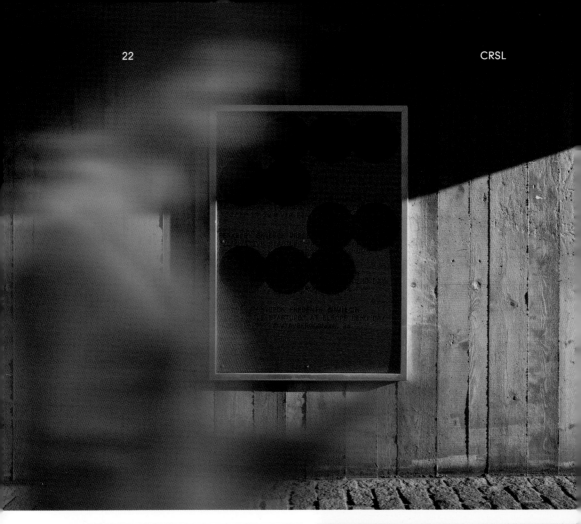

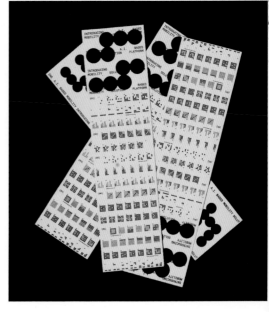

Switch
—
Identity for an artificial intelligence
& machine learning company
2022

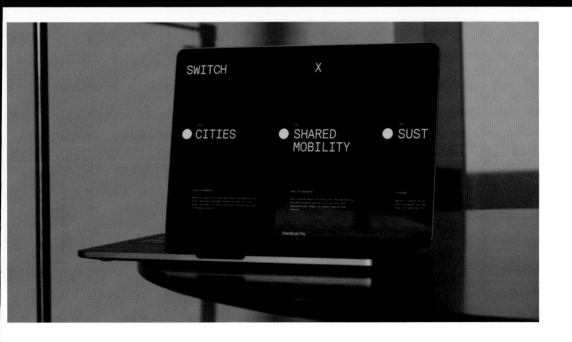

Designers Against Coronavirus

Self-initiated editorial project,
in collaboration with the
Italian Red Cross
2020

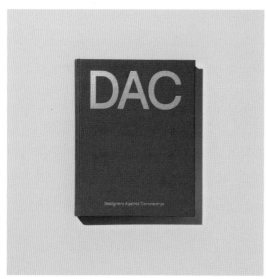

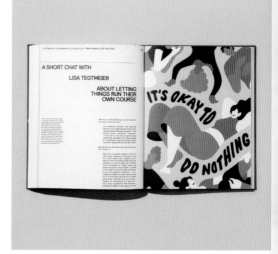

Matteo Vandelli

Orizzonti alti

Rassegna di incontri dedicati alla fotografia

Associazione Antermoia
Campitello–Mazzin 2019

From Italy

matteovandelli.com

Associazione Antermoia

Poster designs for a cultural association

2019 – 2022

Orizzonti alti

Rassegna di incontri
dedicati alla fotografia

Associazione Antermoia
Campitello–Mazzin 2020

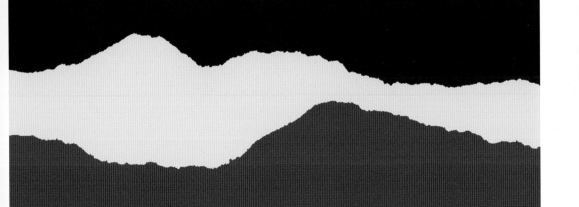

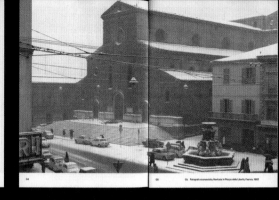

Le origini della Fototeca Manfrediana: custodire la memoria visiva della città

L'Associazione Culturale Fototeca Manfrediana: fotografia a 360 gradi

L'Archivio Fototeca Manfrediana: un patrimonio da valorizzare

Archivio Fototeca Manfrediana

afm

Matteo Vandelli

Arena Borghesi
Editorial & poster designs
for a cinema
2019

Arena Borghesi

Poster design for a cinema
2020

Notturno

Arena
Borghesi
Cinema

edizione straordinaria
estate 2020
piazza Nenni (già della Molinella)
Faenza

info e programma completo su arenaborghesi.it

Italiano

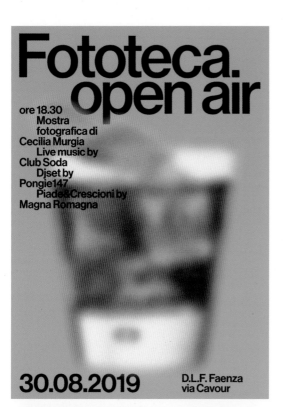

Matteo Vandelli

Fototeca Manfrediana
Poster designs for a cultural
association
2019

→

Fototeca Manfrediana
Poster design for a cultural
association
2020

Fototeca.
open air

ore 18.30
Mostra
fotografica di
Cecilia Murgia
Live music by
Club Soda
Djset by
Pongie147
Piade&Crescioni by
Magna Romagna

30.08.2019   D.L.F. Faenza
via Cavour

Fototeca.
open air

ore 18.30
Mostra
fotografica di
Anna Castaldi
Djset by
Il Baffo
Cold drinks
& Pizza party

31.05.2019   D.L.F. Faenza
via Cavour

Fototeca.
open air

ore 18.30
Mostra
fotografica di
Elena Negri
Djset by
Tommy from Riva
Pregierie veg
di Ravegan

28.06.2019   D.L.F. Faenza
via Cavour

Fototeca. open air

dalle ore 18.30
D.L.F. Faenza
ingresso via Cavour

dj set by Il Baffo
cold drinks
& pizza party

mostra fotografica di
Matteo Cicinelli
Andrea Lauciello
Valerio Visani

31.07.2020

Fototeca Manfrediana
***
Poster design for a cultural association
2018

Fiera di Santa Lucia
Poster design for a local fair
2020

Associazione Antermoia
Editorial design for a cultural
association
2021

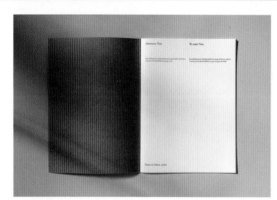

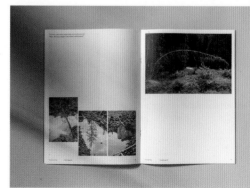

Maxim Dosca

Slanted. Poster design for a print magazine. 2020.

From Italy

maximdosca.com

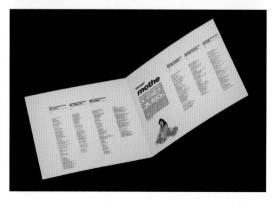

Kilo Kish

Poster & vinyl design for an
American singer-songwriter
2018

→
Unseen Forms
Self-initiated editorial project
2020

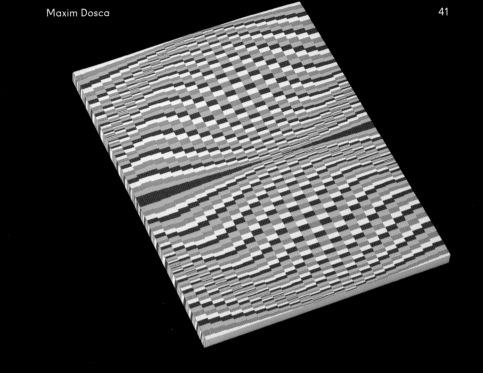

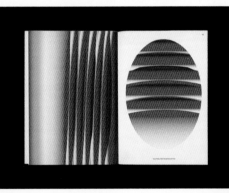

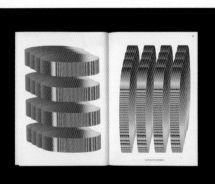

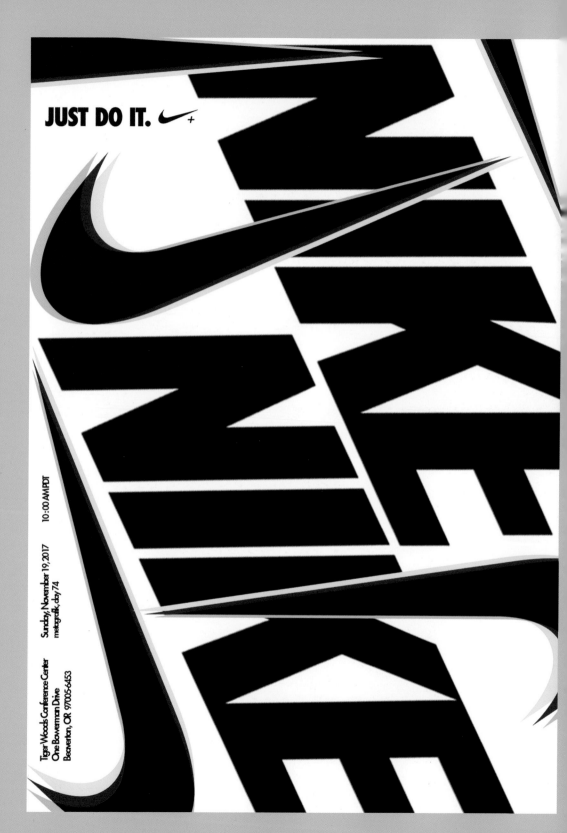

JUST DO IT.

10:00 AM PDT

Sunday, November 19, 2017
metcgolfx, day 74

Tiger Woods Conference Center
One Bowerman Drive
Beaverton, OR 97005-6453

365 Days of Poster

Self-initiated poster designs
2018 – 2020

→

Slanted

Poster design for a print magazine
2020

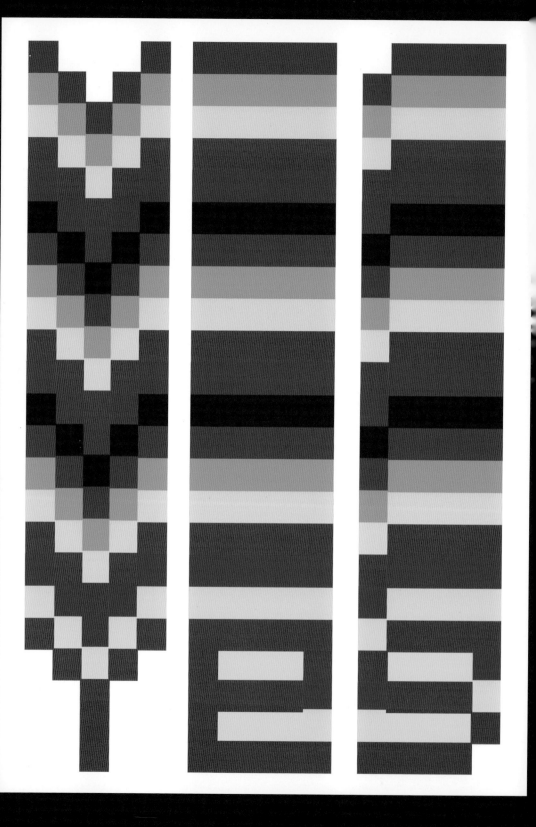

BRH+

From Italy

brh.it

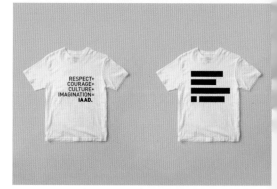

IAAD

Identity for the Institute of Applied Arts & Design
2015 – 2022

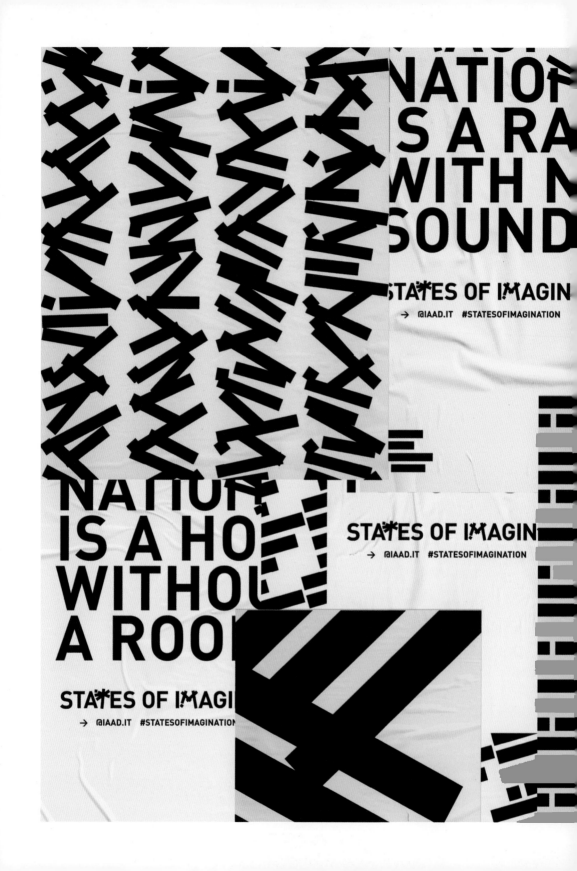

Cabaret Typographie

From Italy.

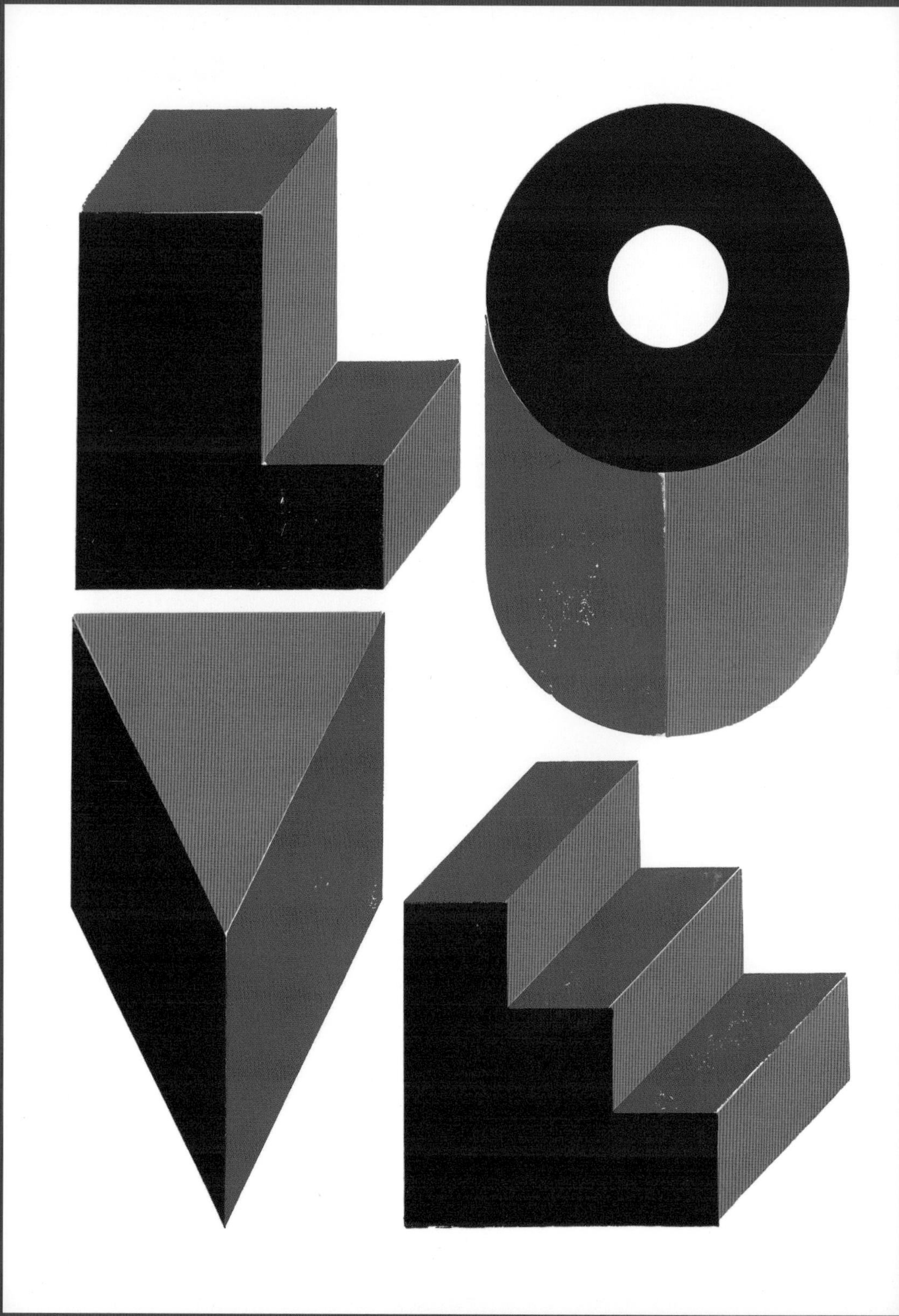

Love
Letterpress poster printed from
digitally designed and laser-cut
wooden matrices. Inspired by the
work of American Pop Art artist
Robert Indiana.
2020

Modernist
Letterpress poster in tribute to
the work of American graphic
designer Alvin Lustig
2022

Peace
Letterpress poster in tribute
to the work of Robert Indiana
2021

→
Milano
Letterpress poster inspired by the
wall-decoration of the Albergo
Diurno Venezia, designed by
architect Piero Portaluppi
2021

→
Venezia
Letterpress poster. The composition,
as well as the design of the letters
of the alphabets, draw inspiration
from the design of Carlo Scarpa
and his decoration of the Querini
Stampalia Foundation's floor.
2021

Spritz
Letterpress poster printed from
digitally designed and laser-cut
wooden matrices. Inspired
by the artist Fortunato Depero
who collaborated with Campari
in the 1920s.
2021

La Tigre

Freely inspired by the Universal Declaration of Human Rights
Article one, Article two and Article three.

AL ORIGIN, PROPERTY, BIRTH OR OTHER STATUS. EVERYONE HAS THE RIGHT TO LIFE, LIBERTY & SECURITY OF PERSON. PEOPLE SHOULD ACT TOWARDS ONE ANOTHER IN A SPIRIT OF BROTHERHOOD. ALL H

ON OF ANY KINDS SUCH AS RACE, COLOUR, SEX, LANGUAGE, RELIGION, POLITICAL OR OTHER OPINION, NATIONAL OR SOCI

OUT DISTINCTIO

ALL HUMAN BEINGS ARE BORN FREE & EQUAL IN DIGNITY AND RIGHTS. WITHO

From Italy

latigre.net

200+ Places & T

Wow Milano

Editorial design for food
blogger Gnambox
2017

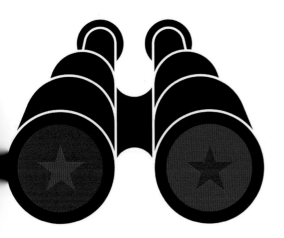

The New York Times Midterm Elections

Illustrations for a newspaper
2018

Art Direction by Deanna Donegano

BRDL BRDL
BRDL BRDL
BRDL BRDL
BRDL BRDL
BRDL

BORDEL
BORDEL
BOR

Bordel Studio
Creative Consultancy

Giacomo Brivio
Partner & Art Director
giacomo@bordel-studio.com
+39 346 038 0792

Via Vincenzo Vela 1, 20133 Milan – Italy
www.bordel.studio

BORDEL
BORDEL
BORDEL

BORDEL
BORDEL
BORDEL

Bordel Studio
Creative Consultancy

Giacomo Brivio
Partner & Art Director
giacomo@bordel-studio.com
+39 346 038 0792

1, 20133 Milan – Italy
l.studio

Bordel Studio
Creative Consultancy

Headquarters
Via Vincenzo Vela 1, 20133 Milan – Italy

Registered Office
Viale Stelvio 20, 20159 Milan – Italy

VAT No. IT08838210964

info@bordel-studio.com
www.bordel.studio

Bordel Studio
Branding for a creative studio
& production agency
2018

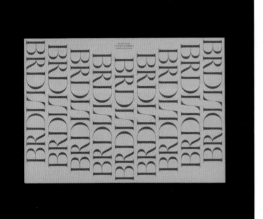

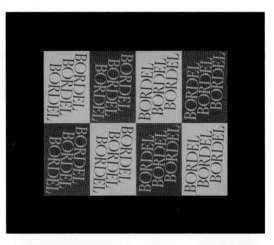

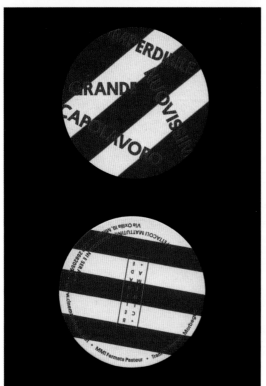

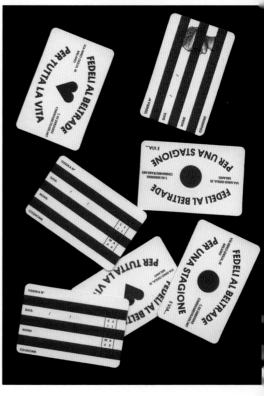

Cinema Beltrade

Branding for a cinema
2015

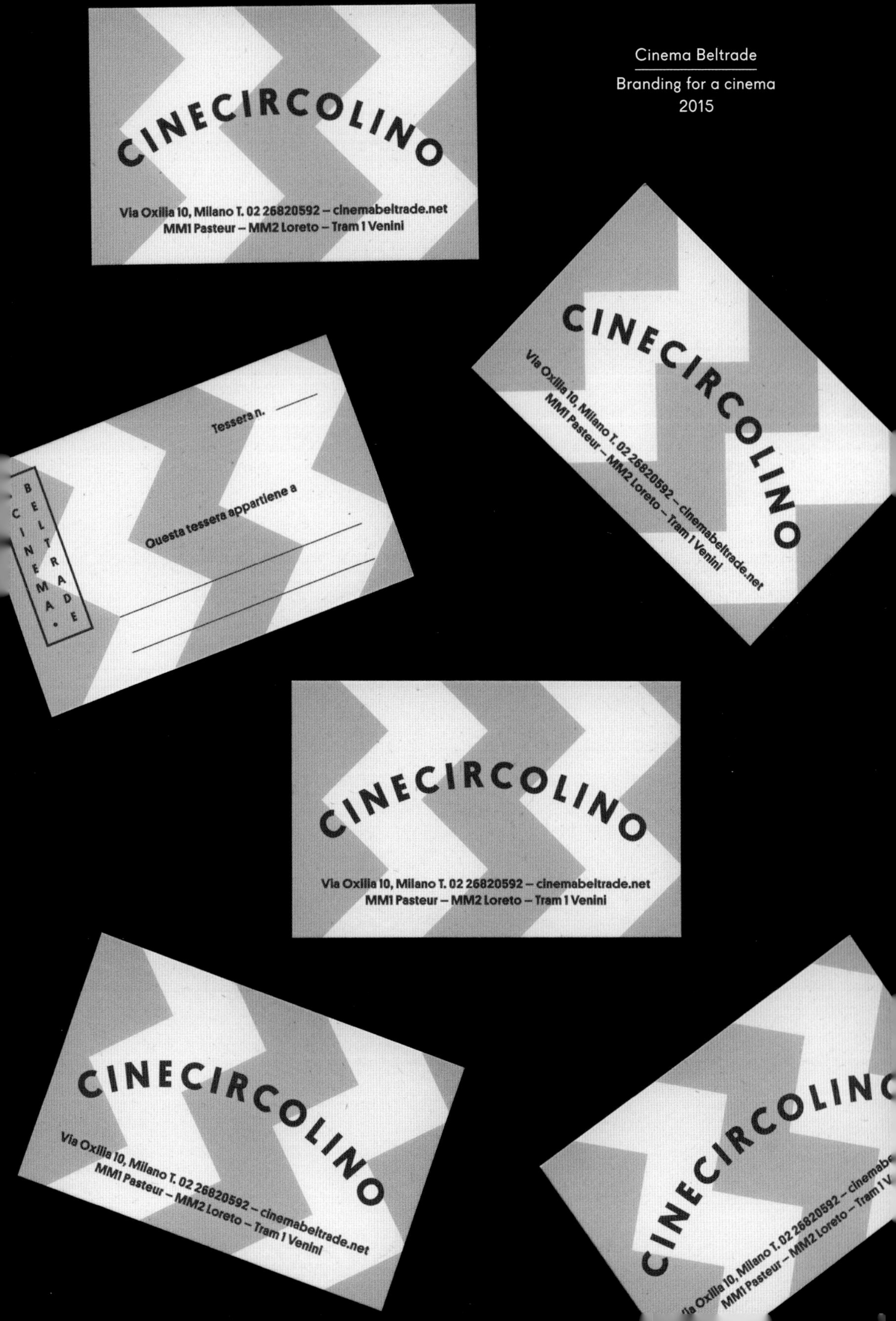

San Marino Republic Stamps

Stamp designs
2017

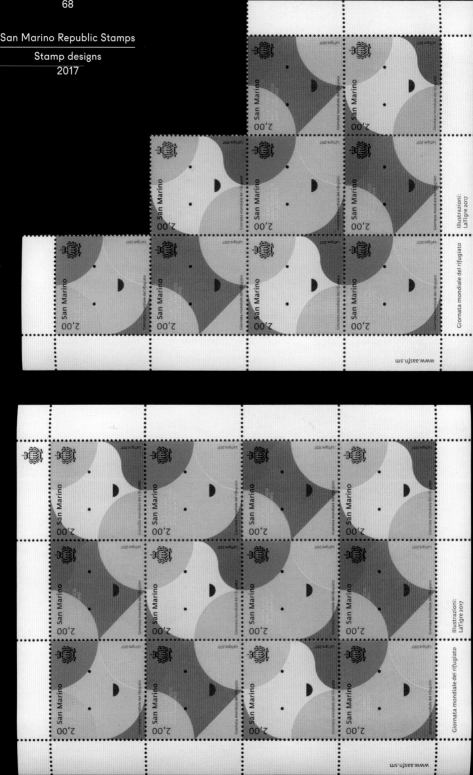

Happycentro

Architettiverona. Editorial design for Ordine Architetti di Verona – special thanks to Alberto Vignolo, 2020.

From Italy

happycentro.it

Architettiverona
———————
Editorial design for Ordine
Architetti di Verona – special
thanks to Alberto Vignolo
2020

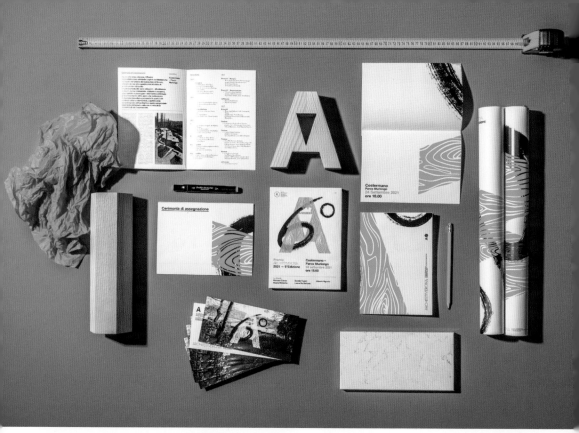

Architettiverona

Identity for the Ordine Architetti
di Verona prize — special thanks
to Alberto Vignolo
2015 – 2021

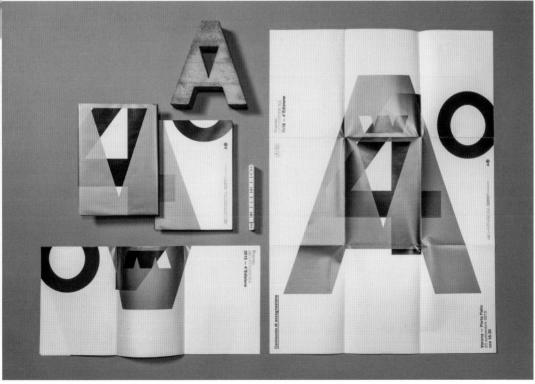

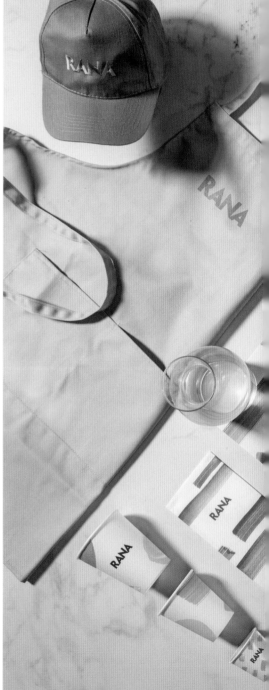

RANA
—
Branding for a pasta factory
& restaurant
2020

Architettura — Bardolino
LA COSTRUZIONE DI UNA NUOVA IDENTITÀ
PER IL TERRITORIO GARDESANO

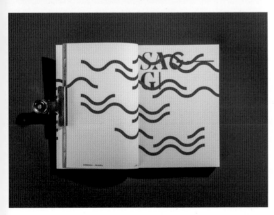

Bardolino Architettura

Editorial design for Comune di Bardolino — Lago di Garda —
Verona, Italy — special thanks to Alberto Vignolo
2021

Feletti – Crema del Commendatore

Packaging design for a
confectionery company
2020

Multi Form

From Italy

multi-form.it

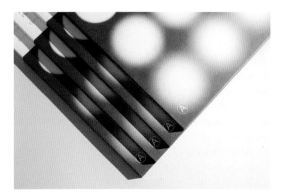

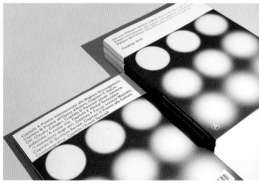

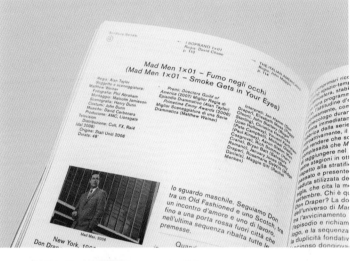

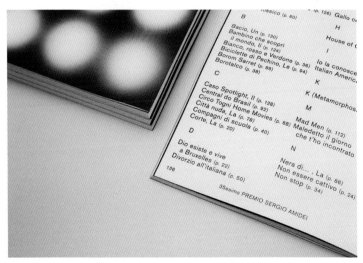

37th Premio Sergio Amidei

Editorial design for Associazione
Sergio Amidei
2016

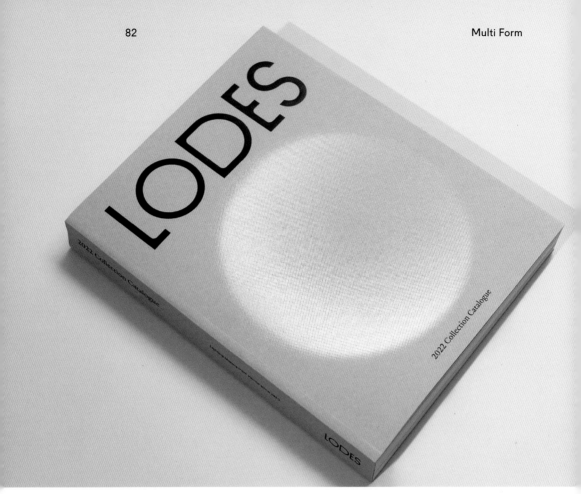

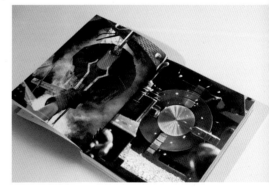

Lodes
—
Editorial design for a lighting brand
2022

Multi Form

9th Biennial Architecture Premio

Marcello D'Olivo

Editorial design for Associazione
Arte & Architettura
2019

Tacchini Italia Forniture

Editorial design for a furniture brand
2019 – 2020

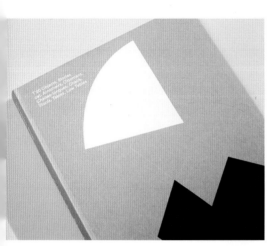

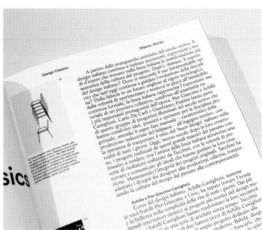

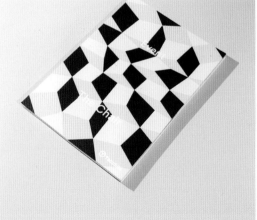

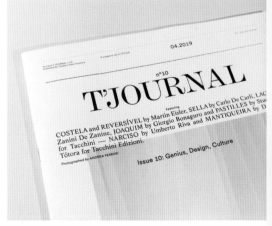

Tacchini Italia Forniture

Editorial design for a furniture brand
2019 – 2020

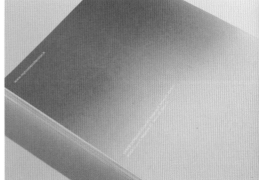

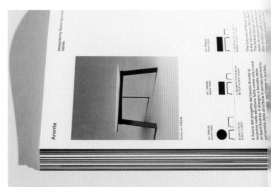

MyHome
Editorial design for a furniture brand
2019

Atto

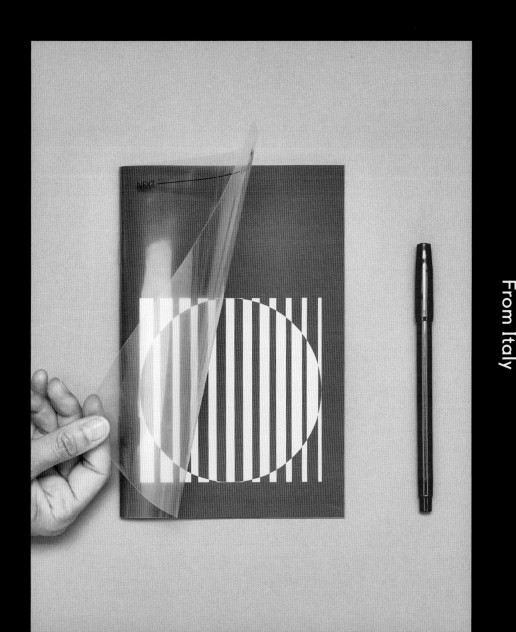

Next Family Wealth. Branding for a wealth advisory boutique. 2019.

From Italy

Next Family Wealth

Branding for a wealth
advisory boutique
2019

Many Possible Cities
———
Identity for a festival about urban
regeneration powered by
Manifattura Tabacchi
2022

Exhibition curated by orizzontale

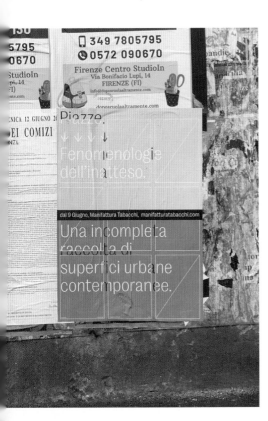

Many Possible Cities

Catalogue design for a festival
about urban regeneration powered
by Manifattura Tabacchi
2022

Catalogue curated by orizzontale

NABA

Identities for an awards programme
on behalf of Nuova Accademia
di Belle Arti
2020 – 2021

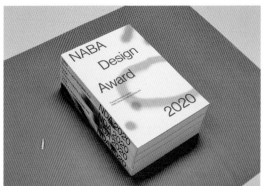

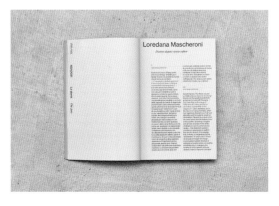

Atto

NABA
Identity for an awards programme
on behalf of Nuova Accademia
di Belle Arti
2022

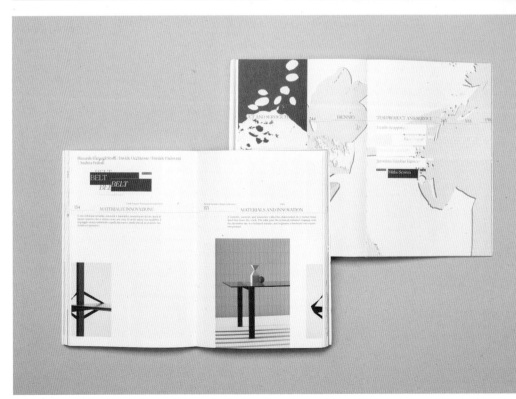

CamuffoLab

Triennale Estate. Identity for 'Collecting Stories', a cultural programme of events. 2022.

From Italy

camuffolab.com

Gusto! Italiani a tavola. 1970-2050

Exhibition identity for Museo M9

2022

Diceva Ennio Flaiano che il nostro, più che u[n]
popolo, è una collezione. Ma quando scocca
l'ora del pranzo, seduti davanti a un piatto
di spaghetti, gli abitanti della penisola si
riconoscono italiani come quelli d'oltre mani[ca]
all'ora del tè, si riconoscono inglesi. L'unità
d'Italia sognata dai padri del Risorgimento o[ra]
si chiama pastasciutta

Si svuotino gli arsenali,
si colmino i granai

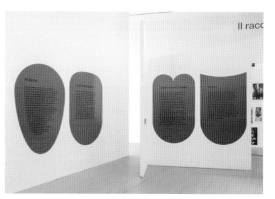

CamuffoLab

TDMX. Giro Giro Tondo.
Design for Children.
Exhibition design for the
Triennale Milano
2016

Photography by Gianluca Di Ioia

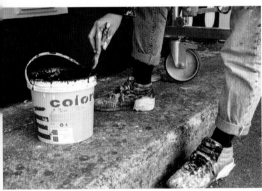

Molla9
Mascot design for M9 Kids
2022

Quando la città cambia tu guarda
i suoi colori
Mural design for the Certosa district
2021

Icaro Hotel
Branding for a hotel
2020

Olimpia Zagnoli

From Italy

olimpiazagnoli.com

PRICE $8.99

THE

NEW YORKER

AUG. 5 & 12, 2019

←

New Yorker
————
'A taste of summer' cover for
August 5&12 issue of The New
Yorker dedicated to summer
2019

New Yorker
————
'Heartfelt' cover for June 24th
issue of The New Yorker dedicated
to Pride
2019

Caleidoscopica
Solo exhibition at Chiostri di San
Pietro, Reggio Emilia curated
by Melania Gazzotti & produced
by Palazzo Magnani
2021

Photography by Miro Zagnoli

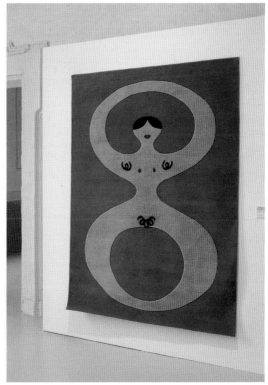

MoMA
Design Store
Pop-Up

Olimpia Zagnoli

FATTO
BENE

←
Italia
Tote design for Fattobene on the
occasion of their pop-up store at
MoMA Design Store in New York
2019

Illy
'Sisters' series of espresso &
cappuccino cups for a coffee brand
2019

→
Eataly
Design for Eataly ice cream & pizza
stand in New York City
2020

Olimpia Zagnoli

←
Moleskine
Cover for a Moleskine notebook
2020

Cavalli e Nastri
Collaboration with graphic designer
Raissa Pardini for a boutique
2019

Tempo
—
Series of eight characters
for a tissue brand
2019

Tassinari/Vetta

From Italy

tassinarivetta.it

Trilogia del Parco Archeologico del Colosseo

Book design & packaging for Electa

2019

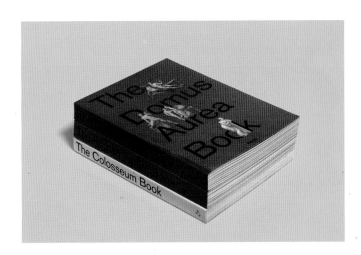

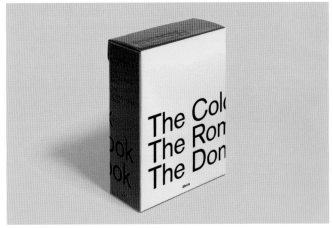

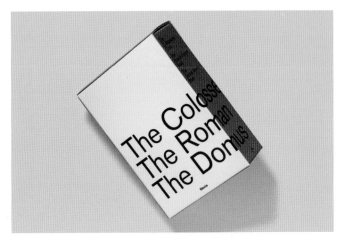

VITTORIA
ALATA
BRESCIA
2020

"Non ho visto nulla di più bello"
Aspettando la Vittoria Alata

Presentazione delle iniziative
per le celebrazioni della Vittoria Alata

Brescia
Palazzo della Loggia, Salone Vanvitelliano
14 novembre 2019, ore 17.30

Intervengono:
Marcello Barbanera, Francesca Bazoli, Stefano
Bucci, Laura Castelletti, Marco Ciatti, Pierre-Alain
Croset, Emilio Del Bono, Emilio Ingrò, Stefano
Karadjov, Francesca Morandini, Juan Navarro
Baldeweg, Alfred Seiland, Paolo Tassinari.

La serata vedrà la presentazione in forma
di lettura scenica di un estratto dello spettacolo
evento Calma musa immortale. Sulle orme della
Vittoria Alata che sarà realizzato dal Centro
Teatrale Bresciano a Brixia. Parco archeologico
di Brescia romana nei giorni del ritorno in città
della Vittoria Alata. Lettura scenica a cura
di Fausto Cabra, testo di Marco Archetti.

"Non ho visto nulla di più bello"
Aspettando la Vittoria Alata

Brescia, Palazzo della Loggia
14 novembre 2019, ore 17.30

Brescia vola sulle ali
della Vittoria. Nel nuovo
Capitolium disegnato
da Juan Navarro Baldeweg
una dea romana in bronzo

Vittoria Alata Brescia 2020

Book design, communication, digital, identity & packaging for Fondazione Brescia Musei 2020

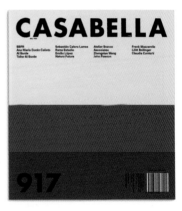

Casabella

Art direction & editorial design
for Arnoldo Mondadori Editore
1996 – 2023

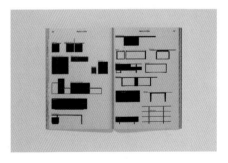

The World of Tecno
——————————
Book design for a furniture brand
2020

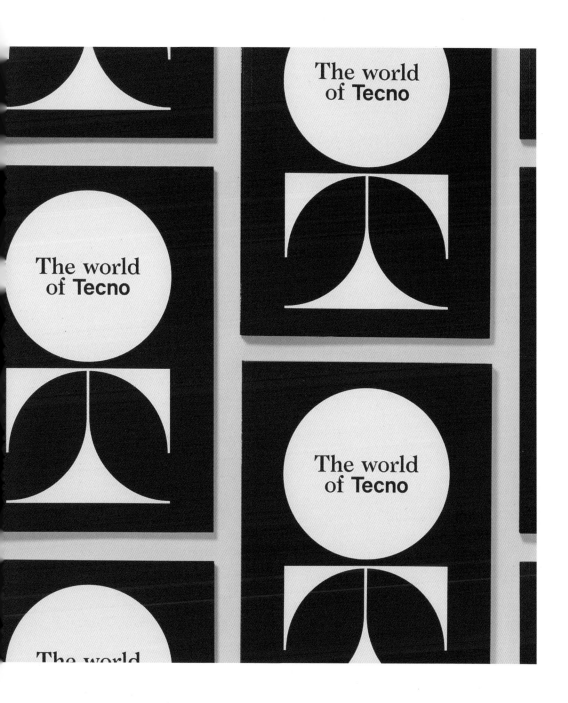

SISSA Scienza e Virgola

Identity design for SISSA — Scuola
Superiore di Studi Avanzati
2021

Ma   Pà
Maa   Pàà
Maa a   Pàà à
Ma   Pà
Maa aaa   Pàà ààà
Ma a   Pà à
Ma a a   Pà à à
Maaaaaa   Pààààààà
Maternità   Paternità

Votate   Votate   Votate Si può fare
Votate   Votate   Votate

per la famiglia

Votate SI Votate SI   al congedo
Votate SI Votate SI

di Paternità

Votate SI Votate SI   il 20.04.2019
Votate SI Votate SI

ECAL/University of Art and Design Lausanne. Poster for an art & design university 2018

From Italy

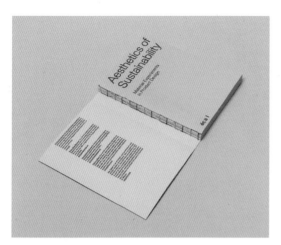

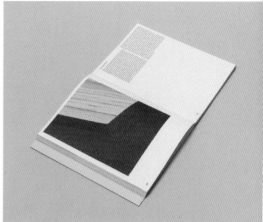

←

ECAL/University of
Art and Design Lausanne
Editorial design for an art
& design university
2021

Photography by Vincent Levrat

Villa Filanda Antonini
Editorial design for an art gallery
2022

Photography by Giulio Boem

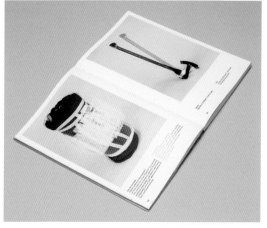

Federico Barbon

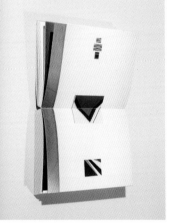

ISBN 978-88-7490-335-1

Michele Lombardelli
UNTITLED

UNTITLED

Michele Lombardelli

postmediabooks
MA*GA

ECAL/University of
Art and Design Lausanne
Editorial design for an art
& design university
2019

Photography by Vincent Levrat

Michele Lombardelli
Editorial design for a painter
2022

Photography by Vincent Levrat

ECAL/University of Art
and Design Lausanne
Poster design for an art
& design university
2021

Junior

Design

Research

Conference

ECAL / FHNW / HEAD / HKB / HSLU / ZHDK

18 November 2021

éc a l   www.ecal.ch

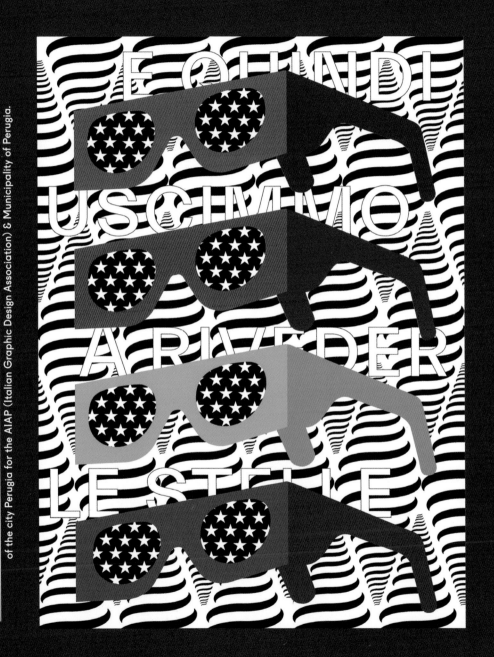

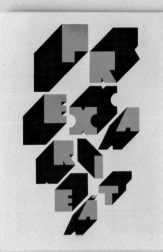

Mauro Bubbico / Marzia Bric

Inaugurazione
Matera — Palazzo Lanfranchi
— mercoledi 16 settembre
ore 20.30 – 21.00 – 21.30
Lali Ayguade, Incognito
Francisco Cordova Azuela,
Postskriptum Gil Kerer, Beetwen Us
— Prenotazione obbligatoria
Telefonare alla Segreteria org. 348 5655627

Potenza — Teatro Francesco Stabile
— giovedi 17 settembre — ore 20.30
La Veronal / Marcos Morau, Shortcuts
— Prima nazionale

Potenza — Teatro Francesco Stabile
1 ottobre – 14 dicembre

Enzo Cosimi, Leonardo Delogu e Valerio Sirna / Dom-,
Motus, Maurizio Saiu, Jan Fabre_Troubleyn,
Nicola Galli, Kinkaleri, Societas Raffaelo Sanzio
_Freddanotte, Antonio Latella, Factory Compagnia
Transadriatica, Collettivo Cinetico, Virgilio Sieni,
Balletto Civile, Babilonia Teatri, Gommalacca Teatro,
Giulio D'anna_Fattoria Vittadini, Emma Dante,
Compagnia Teatrale Petra, Compagnia Abito in Scena,
Officina Accademia Teatro, Fortebraccio Teatro
_Roberto Latini, Vico Quarto Mazzini

Matera
— Potenza
16 sett —
14 dic
— 2015

Matera
— Potenza
16 sett —
14 dic
— 2015
Rassegna
internazionale
di danza
urbana
e arte
performativa
nei paesaggi
urbani

**FESTIVAL
CITTÂ
DELLE 100
SCALE**

**FESTIVAL
CITTÂ
DELLE 100
SCALE**

Rassegna
internazionale
di danza
urbana e arte
performativa
nei paesaggi
urbani

City of a Hundred Stairs Festival

Identity for Association Basilicata
1799, a cultural association
2015

CARTACANTA FESTIVAL

LA RIPARTENZA
28.9—
—12.12.2021
CIVITA
NOVA
MARCHE

MUSEO MAGMA
PALAZZINA LIDO CLUANA
SPAZIO MULTIMEDIALE
SAN FRANCESCO

AIAP IMPRESA

CARTA

CMA
VIN

REGIONE MARCHE

COMUNE DI CIVITANOVA MARCHE

←
The Restart

Poster design for Association
Cartacanta, a cultural association
2021

Grano e Vite.
La benedizione dei campi
Gravina in Puglia

Festa della focaccia
e della Verdeca Gravinesi
25 maggio 2018

Grano e Vite.
La benedizione dei campi
Gravina in Puglia

Solenni festeggiamenti
in onore del SS. Crocifisso
25 maggio 2018

The Blessing of the Fields

Poster designs for Association SS.
Crocifisso, a cultural association
2018

→
Oi Marì

Branding for a restaurant
2018

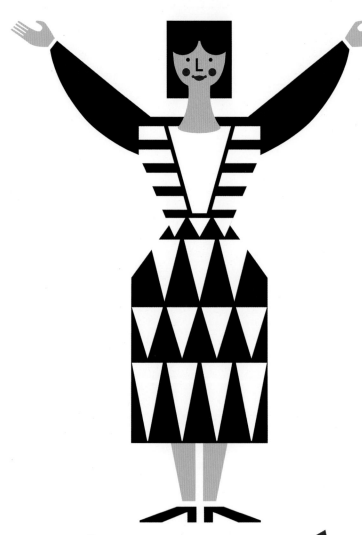

Oi Marì

Multiplo

From Italy

multiplo.biz

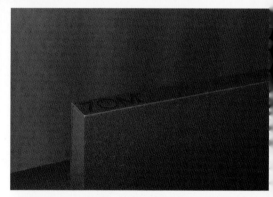

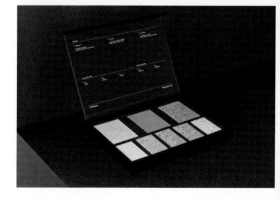

70Materia

Identity for a surface design company
2022

Dalla sapiente commistione di sabbia, cemento e acqua
lavorati al naturale, colorati con pigmenti o impreziositi
da altri materiali nascono tre tipologie di prodotto.

La stessa tipologia declinata in diverse finiture consente
di creare continuità tra applicazioni in interno e in esterno.
La texture, appena accennata nella superficie lamata, diventa
più evidente nelle finiture anticata, levigata e spazzolata,
fino a raggiungere l'effetto pietra della versione bocciardata.

Tipologia		
	○	Origine
	○	Colore
	○	Progetto

Finitura		
	○	Lamato
	○	Anticato
	○	Levigato
	○	Spazzolato
	○	Bocciardato

Mondadori Electa Editore

Editorial design for a publisher
2022

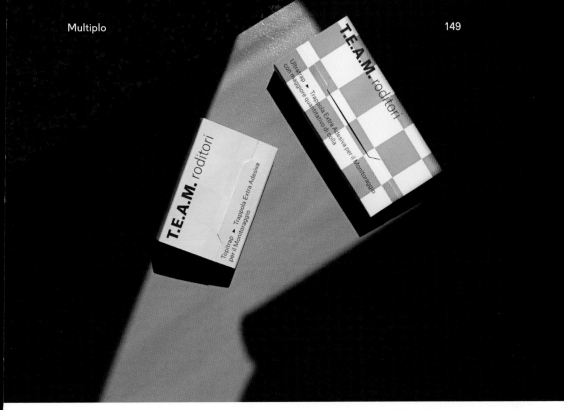

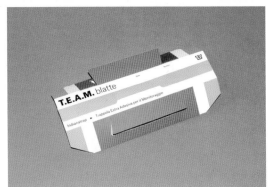

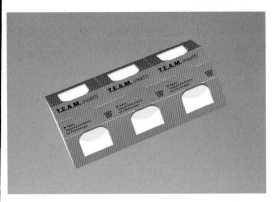

I.N.D.I.A.

Packaging design for a chemical
production company
2021

Eremo

ART 32. Poster design for a cultural association. 2021.

From Italy

eremo.studio

Eremo Landscape

Self-promotional material for
graphic design studio Eremo
2017

→
Torri Lana 1885

Editorial design for an historic
Italian textile factory
2018

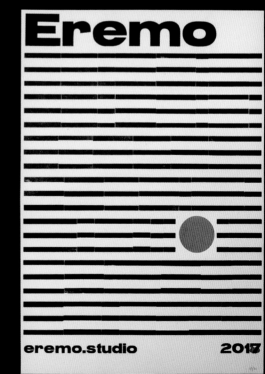

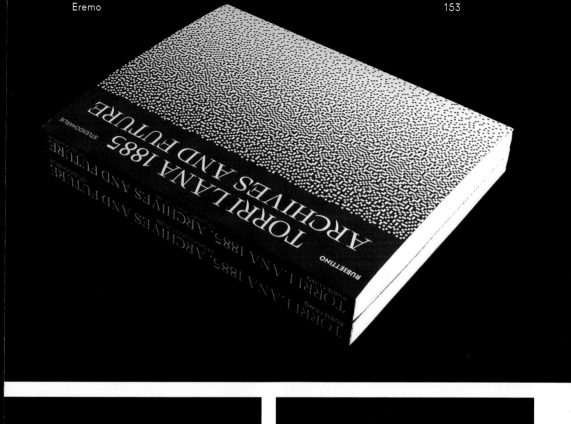

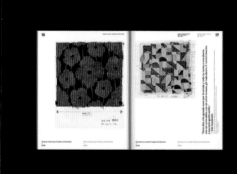

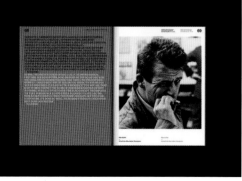

Positional

Journal design for Rubbettino
Editore, an Italian publisher
2020 – 2023

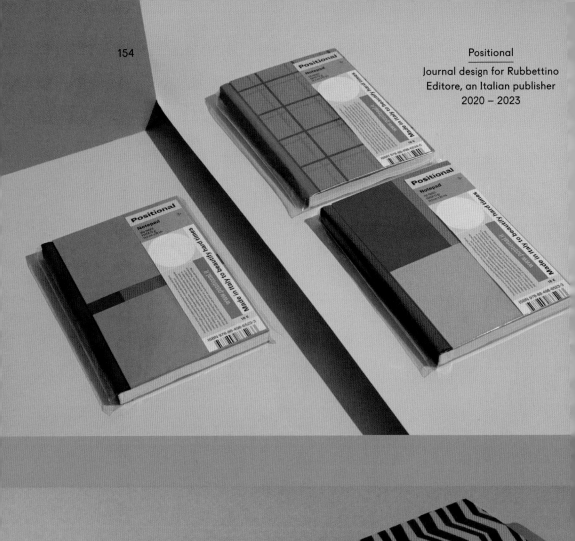

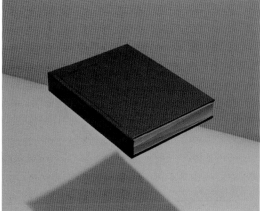

→
Galuppi Architect Studio
Identity for an architecture studio
2020

Dr. Arch. Daniele Galoppi
Fraz. Conferenze 26
10010 Genova
P.IVA 02000030900

M +39 342 80 60 506
danielegaloppi44@gmail.com
IG @daniele_galoppi

ANALISI ENERGETICA
per Proposta di Riqualificazione secondo UNI CEI EN 16247-1-2,
UNI CEI/TR 11428 ed il progetto di linee guida CTI per le diagnosi
energetiche degli edifici.

Edifici

Indirizzo

Committente

Comune

Dr. Arch. Daniele Galoppi
Fraz. Conferenze 26
10010 Genova
P.IVA 02000030900

M +39 342 80 60 506
danielegaloppi44@gmail.com
IG @daniele_galoppi

Dr. Arch. Daniele Galoppi
Fraz. Conferenze 26
10010 Genova
P.IVA 02000030900

M +39 342 80 60 506
danielegaloppi44@gmail.com
IG @daniele_galoppi

RELAZIONE DI CANTIERE

Edifici

Indirizzo

Committente

Comune

Camilla Falsini

Supplemento a VANITY FAIR n. 36 - Settembre 2021

VANITY FAIR
DESIGN

MODELLO MILANO

SOSTENIBILITÀ, TECNOLOGIA, UMANITÀ. PROGETTI IN EVOLUZIONE, INNOVAZIONI E RISCOPERTE, TENDENZE E PROTAGONISTI

From Italy

camillafalsini.it

ARTWORK BY CAMILLA FALSINI

CARNEVALE DI FOIANO DELLA CHIANA (AR)

5 | 12 | 19 | 26 FEBBRAIO | 5 MARZO

Associazione
Carnevale
Foiano della Chiana

Comune di
Foiano della Chiana

MINISTERO
DELLA
CULTURA

REGIONE
TOSCANA

PROVINCIA
DI AREZZO

PER INFO E BIGLIETTI: WWW.CARNEVALEDIFOIANO.IT

CARNEVALE DI FOIANO DELLA CHIANA (AR)
5 | 12 | 19 | 26 FEBBRAIO | 5 MARZO

PER INFO E BIGLIETTI: WWW.CARNEVALEDIFOIANO.IT

Foiano Carnival

Posters & flags designed
for the Foiano Carnival
2022 – 2023

Camilla Falsini

20TH CONCORTO
FILM FESTIVAL
17-24 AUGUST 2021
PONTENURE / PIACENZA ITALY

← Concorto

Posters & flyers designed for a short
movie festival near Piacenza, Italy
2021

Bombay Sapphire

Illustrations for a gin brand
2021 – 2022

Review

IL FOGLIO

30 LUGLIO 2022 ANNO II ~ N. 10

MY
BO

SUPPLEMENTO AL NUMERO ODIERNO DE IL FOGLIO ~ EURO 2 ~ CON IL FOGLIO EURO 0,50

←
Review

Cover illustration for the Review
de IL FOGLIO magazine
2022

'Love Is Love' Gay Pride,
Apple Store

A festival of illustration
in partnership with the
Apple Store in Milan
2022

Pictures also include works by
Riccardo Guasco, Irene Rinaldi
& Francesco Poroli

 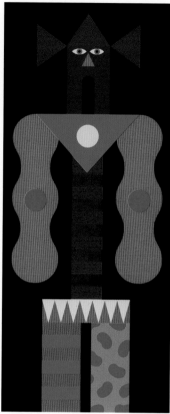 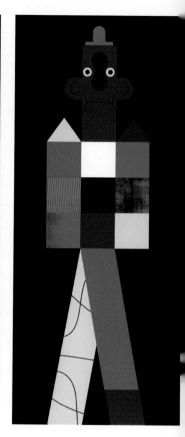

Palazzo Fondi

Illustrations for banners hung in the
historical Palazzo Fondi in Naples
2022

Parco Studio parco.studio

CRSL crsl.studio

Matteo Vandelli matteovandelli.com

Maxim Dosca maximdosca.com

BRH+ brh.it

Cabaret Typographie cabarettypographie.com

La Tigre latigre.net

Happycentro happycentro.it

Multi Form multi-form.it

Atto atto.si

CamuffoLab camuffolab.com

Olimpia Zagnoli olimpiazagnoli.com

Tassinari/Vetta tassinarivetta.it

Federico Barbon federicobarbon.com

Mauro Bubbico maurobubbico.it

Multiplo multiplo.biz

Eremo eremo.studio

Camilla Falsini camillafalsini.it